Will You Be My Friend?

Angela Ramos Fields

Illustrated by:
Freddie Crocheron

ISBN: 978-1-950936-11-3 (Paperback)
ISBN: 978-1-950936-12-0 (E-book)
Library of Congress Control Number: 2019908604

Edited by: Laurel J. Davis
Illustrations and Cover Design: Freddie Crocheron
Literary Director: Sandra L. Slayton

Published by:
KP Publishing Company
A Division of Knowledge Power Communications, Inc.
Valencia, CA 91355
www.kp-pub.com

Printed in the United States of America

I lovingly dedicate this book to my sons;
Blaize and Grant Fields.

Hello! My name is Sam. I'm six-years old and I live with my Mom, Dad and big brother.

Most days I'm happy with my family. We eat and play together. I feel safe at home.

My big brother is like
a superhero to me.

He's kind, protective and fun.
His superpowers are amazing.

I go to school and I do amazing things that make me feel like a big boy. I love reading about rockets and drawing pictures of spaceships. One day, I want to be an astronaut.

School is fun, but some days are harder than others. I have autism. Do you know what autism is? Autism means I think differently.

Sometimes sounds, colors, lights and different places make me feel uncomfortable.

I cannot help how I act. Learning to manage my frustration is hard but I put my best effort everyday. I can't control my behavior like other children. I might have a meltdown which looks like a tantrum.

My meltdowns are results from my frustration. The behaviors I have are because of my autism. I will have autism for the rest of my life.

Other boys and girls think I am strange and they make fun of me. This hurts my feelings and I feel bad. At the park or on the playground I get bullied.

Some boys and girls think I am too different and will not be my friend. I know that having autism makes me different but I think being different makes me wonderful. We are all different. We all are wonderful in our own special way.

For instance, there is a girl in my class with red hair and a boy in my class with green eyes. All of us are different. All of us are wonderful.

It is not nice to bully people. If I could make a wish it would be for all the children to stop making fun of me. I wish they could just see how well I can read and draw.

I wish they knew how much I love space, rockets and spaceships. I wish they could see that I'm a nice person and want to be part of the group. In fact, I wish no one would get pushed or ignored. No one would get bullied.

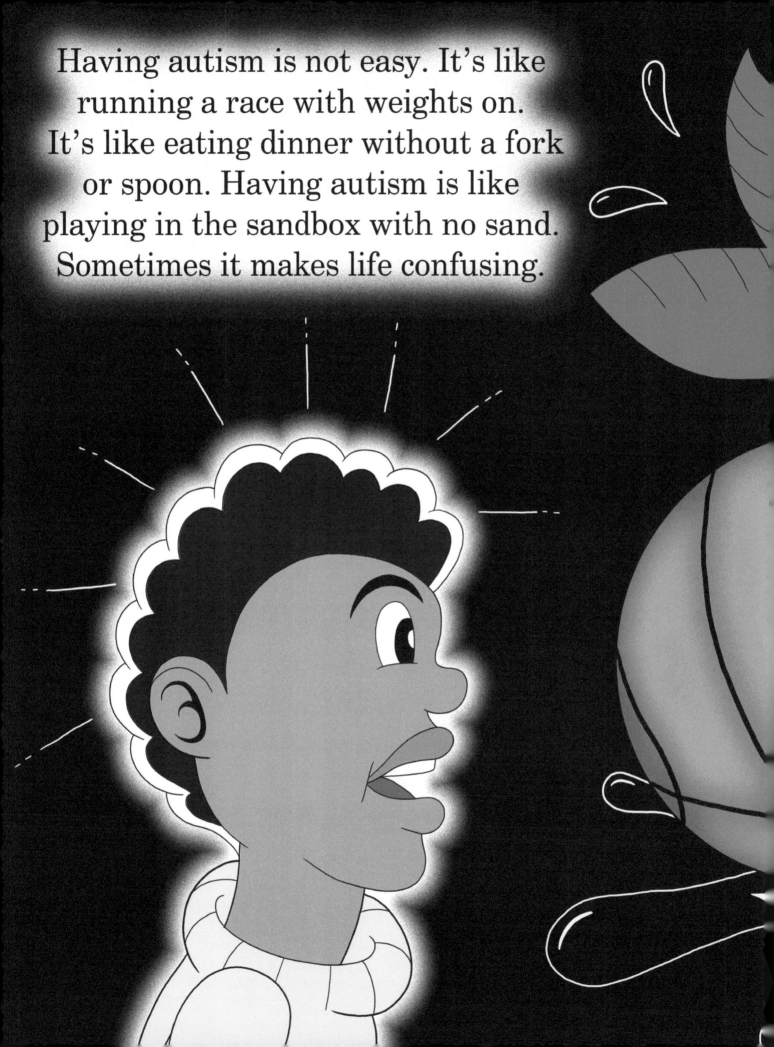

Having autism is not easy. It's like running a race with weights on. It's like eating dinner without a fork or spoon. Having autism is like playing in the sandbox with no sand. Sometimes it makes life confusing.

Other times autism is like looking at a beautiful color like blue for the first time. It's like tasting something sweet magnified by 100. Senses can either make things confusing or amazing.

Like having my brother as my best friend, reading a new book about spaceships, going to school and seeing my favorite teachers. All of those things are fun.

Having friends that are different is fun too. My last wish is to have more friends.

About the Author

Angela Ramos Fields is the creator of the character, Samuel, a six-year old boy with autism. She is the mother of two sons and was inspired and motivated by her youngest son's diagnosis of Autism Spectrum Disorder (ASD) to create two non-profit organizations, Living Beyond Autism and Emerging Autism Solutions (EAS). Ms. Fields is the president of Emerging Autism Solutions (EAS), headquartered in Columbus, Ohio. She has served on several executive committees and taskforces for autism related organizations. Her mission quickly evolved to connecting families together to learn advocacy strategies and tactical practices. A graduate of Ohio Wesleyan University and in her free time, she enjoys being with family and friends and speaking on various autism topics throughout Ohio and beyond.

Acknowledgements

There are have many people that encouraged and supported me as I wrote this book. I would like to acknowledge each of you. Please know you are appreciated even if I did not mention you by name.

I want to recognize my sons, Blaize and Grant Fields. They have served as my motivation and inspiration in which propelled me to have the vision for this book. I'm grateful, and I love you both so much. I would like to thank my mother, Audrey Holmes, for her unyielding support throughout my life. With her love, I was able to start and finish this project.

My siblings. Sylvester Holmes, Rose Minton, Joseph Holmes, Audrey Hamilton, and Ahmad Holmes, thank you for the countless group text messages that included pictures, words of encouragement and love. To my fellow autism moms, Elaine Hamilton and Toni Johnson, 100 thank yous! You know the fight, persistence, and dedication that is needed to exist in this community. Thank you for always being there.

My girlfriends, Darla Ball, Rosemary Duffy Copper, Denise Hayes, Carla Granger, and Lavern "Shay" Thomas, I can't thank you enough for all the cheers, direction and presence in my life! I have some of the best friends in the world.

Thank you to the daughter I always wanted, Milan McMullen. Your insight and feedback were always amazing.

To Chad South and my entire work family, thank you for being my soundboard.

To the incredible illustrator, Freddie Crocheron thank you for making my vision a reality. Samuel is real because of you.

To William Derrick, you continue to inspire me. Thank you for your love and support during this project. I'm blessed to have you.

And finally, thank you to Dr. Donna Hunter. You believe in giving so willingly. You certainly carry the torch. Eternally grateful.

What is Autism?

According to the American Psychiatric Association autism is defined as follows: Autism spectrum disorder (ASD) is a complex developmental condition that involves persistent challenges in social interaction, speech and nonverbal communication, and restricted/repetitive behaviors. The effects of ASD and the severity of symptoms are different in each person.

A child or adult with autism spectrum disorder may have problems with social interaction and communication skills, including any of these signs:

- Fails to respond to his or her name
- Resists cuddling and holding
- Strong preference to play alone
- Has poor eye contact
- Doesn't speak or has delayed speech
- Doesn't initiate a conversation
- Regression in learned language or skill
- Doesn't appear to understand simple questions or directions
- Doesn't understand emotions
- Inappropriately approaches a social interaction by being passive, aggressive or disruptive

If you have concerns or questions, consult your medical doctor.

What is Bullying?

Bullying is a repeat, negative unwanted action towards another individual. There is usually an imbalance of perceived power between the bully and the victim. There are several types of bullying:

- **Verbal Bullying**
  - Calling someone names
  - Teasing
  - Taunting
  - Threating to harm someone
- **Social Bullying**
  - Purposefully leaving someone out
  - Encouraging others not to be friends with someone
  - Lying about someone
  - Embarrassing someone in public
- **Physical Bullying**
  - Hitting
  - Kicking
  - Spitting
  - Pushing
  - Taking or breaking things that belong to others

What should you do if you have been bullied?
- **Tell some one.**
  - Tell your parents, teachers or adults

Don't let bulling define you.
Continue to treat everyone with kindness and respect.